FRANCIS FRITH'S

SUFFOLK VILLAGES

PHOTOGRAPHIC MEMORIES

CLIVE PAINE was born and educated in Bury St Edmunds, and apart
from his years at university has worked there all his life. He is a teacher,
lecturer, author and broadcaster on all aspects of local history. He has
taught history and local history for 30 years, 21 of which were as County
Advisory Teacher for Archives and Local History in Suffolk. He has been
a part-time lecturer in Local History for the Cambridge University
Institute of Continuing Education for over 20 years. His publications
include *Hartest: A Village History*; *The Culford Estate, The History of Eye,
The Spoil of Melford Church* (with David Dymond); *Francis Frith's Bury
St Edmunds, The Suffolk Bedside Book*, and *Francis Frith's Suffolk*. He
frequently broadcasts on local and national radio, and he appeared with
Prince Edward on his *Crown and Country* series for ITV; he has also
been profiled in *Reader's Digest*. He is a Council member of the Suffolk
Institute of Archaeology and History and the Executive of the Suffolk
Local History Council, and he is past Chairman of the Education
Committee of the British Association for Local History. He is also a Lay
Reader at St Mary's in Bury.

FRANCIS FRITH'S
PHOTOGRAPHIC MEMORIES

SUFFOLK VILLAGES

PHOTOGRAPHIC MEMORIES

CLIVE PAINE

First published in the United Kingdom in 2003 by
Frith Book Company Ltd

Hardback Edition 2003
ISBN 1-85937-666-5

British Library Cataloguing in Publication Data

Suffolk Villages - Photographic Memories
Clive Paine

Frith Book Company Ltd
Frith's Barn, Teffont,
Salisbury, Wiltshire SP3 5QP
Tel: +44 (0) 1722 716 376
Email: info@francisfrith.co.uk
www.francisfrith.co.uk

Printed and bound in Great Britain

Front Cover: **KERSEY**, *Kersey Street c1965* K136042
Frontispiece: **BOTESDALE**, *The Village c1955* B619001

Acknowledgements

In preparing the captions I have visited every location and met so many friendly and generous people who shared their local knowl-
edge and memories. I wish especially to thank the following for their essential contributions to the book: Alan Benton, Evelyn
Bloomfield, Len Boreham, June Brereton, Barbara Caruth, Mary Chilvers, Margaret and Anthony Collins, John Cummins, Michael
Earey, Jim Fenning, Jean Folkard, Marjorie Frape, Wendy Gillings, Mary and Hedley Goddard, Bob Goodall, Tony Green, Joyce
Hazelwood, Bill Heffer, Ann Henderson, Fiona Johnson, Keith Jonceline, Betty Jordan, Stan Lawrence, Ray Leek, Audrey McLaughlin,
Bob Malster, Jo Pask, Susie and Will Patten, Carol Read, Julia Reisz, Rose Spalding, Ray and David Turner, Robert Webster, Kath
Whatling and Michael Wood.

Many thanks also go to Jane Cummins, who worked miracles from my handwriting to set the text, and to David Caruth, who
painstakingly read the proofs. Any mistake in matters of detail are, of course, mine alone.

CONTENTS

FRANCIS FRITH
VICTORIAN PIONEER

FRANCIS FRITH, founder of the world-famous photographic archive, was a complex and multi-talented man. A devout Quaker and a highly successful Victorian businessman, he was philosophic by nature and pioneering in outlook.

By 1855 he had already established a wholesale grocery business in Liverpool, and sold it for the astonishing sum of £200,000, which is the equivalent today of over £15,000,000. Now a very rich man, he was able to indulge his passion for travel. As a child he had pored over travel books written by early explorers, and his fancy and imagination had been stirred by family holidays to the sublime mountain regions of Wales and Scotland. 'What lands of spirit-stirring and enriching scenes and places!' he had written. He was to return to these scenes of grandeur in later years to 'recapture the thousands of vivid and tender memories', but with a different purpose. Now in his thirties, and captivated by the new science of photography, Frith set out on a series of pioneering journeys up the Nile and to the Near East that occupied him from 1856 until 1860.

INTRIGUE AND EXPLORATION

These far-flung journeys were packed with intrigue and adventure. In his life story, written when he was sixty-three, Frith tells of being held captive by bandits, and of fighting 'an awful midnight battle to the very point of surrender with a deadly pack of hungry, wild dogs'. Wearing flowing Arab costume, Frith arrived at Akaba by camel seventy years before Lawrence of Arabia, where he encountered 'desert princes and rival sheikhs, blazing with jewel-hilted swords'.

He was the first photographer to venture beyond the sixth cataract of the Nile. Africa was still the mysterious 'Dark Continent', and Stanley and Livingstone's historic meeting was a decade into the future. The conditions for picture taking confound belief. He laboured for hours in his wicker dark-room in the sweltering heat of the desert, while the volatile chemicals fizzed dangerously in their trays. Back in London he exhibited his photographs and was 'rapturously cheered' by members of the Royal Society. His reputation as a photographer was made overnight.

VENTURE OF A LIFE-TIME

Characteristically, Frith quickly spotted the opportunity to create a new business as a specialist publisher of photographs. He lived in an era of immense and sometimes violent change.

For the poor in the early part of Victoria's reign work was exhausting and the hours long, and people had precious little free time to enjoy themselves. Most had no transport other than a cart or gig at their disposal, and rarely travelled far beyond the boundaries of their own town or village. However, by the 1870s the railways had threaded their way across the country, and Bank Holidays and half-day Saturdays had been made obligatory by Act of Parliament. All of a sudden the working man and his family were able to enjoy days out and see a little more of the world.

With typical business acumen, Francis Frith foresaw that these new tourists would enjoy having souvenirs to commemorate their days out. In 1860 he married Mary Ann Rosling and set out on a new career: his aim was to photograph every city, town and village in Britain. For the next thirty years he travelled the country by train and by pony and trap, producing fine photographs of seaside resorts and beauty spots that were keenly bought by millions of Victorians. These prints were painstakingly pasted into family albums and pored over during the dark nights of winter, rekindling precious memories of summer excursions.

THE RISE OF FRITH & CO

Frith's studio was soon supplying retail shops all over the country. To meet the demand he gathered about him a small team of photographers, and published the work of independent artist-photographers of the calibre of Roger Fenton and Francis Bedford. In order to gain some understanding of the scale of Frith's business one only has to look at the catalogue issued by Frith & Co in 1886: it runs to some 670 pages, listing not only many thousands of views of the British Isles but also many photographs of most European countries, and China, Japan, the USA and Canada - note the sample page shown on page 9 from the hand-written Frith & Co ledgers recording the pictures. By 1890 Frith had created the greatest specialist photographic publishing company in the world, with over 2,000 sales outlets - more than the combined number that Boots and WH Smith have today! The picture on the next page shows the Frith & Co display board at Ingleton in the Yorkshire Dales (left of window). Beautifully constructed with a mahogany frame and gilt inserts, it could display up to a dozen local scenes.

POSTCARD BONANZA

The ever-popular holiday postcard we know today took many years to develop. In 1870 the Post Office issued the first plain cards, with a pre-printed stamp on one face. In 1894 they allowed other publishers' cards to be sent through the mail with an attached adhesive half-penny stamp. Demand grew rapidly, and in 1895 a new size of postcard was permitted called the court card, but there was little room for illustration. In 1899, a year after Frith's death, a new card measuring 5.5 x 3.5 inches became the standard format, but it was not until 1902 that the divided back came into being, so that the address and message could be on one face and a full-size illustration on the other. Frith & Co were in the vanguard of postcard development: Frith's sons Eustace and Cyril continued their father's monumental task, expanding the number of views offered to the public and recording more and more places in Britain, as the coasts and countryside were opened up to mass travel.

Francis Frith had died in 1898 at his villa in Cannes, his great project still growing. The archive he created continued in business for another seventy years. By 1970 it contained over a third of a million pictures showing 7,000 British towns and villages.

FRANCIS FRITH'S LEGACY

Frith's legacy to us today is of immense significance and value, for the magnificent archive of evocative photographs he created provides a unique record of change in the cities, towns and villages throughout Britain over a century and more. Frith and his fellow studio photographers revisited locations many times down the years to update their views, compiling for us an enthralling and colourful pageant of British life and character.

We are fortunate that Frith was dedicated to recording the minutiae of everyday life. For it is this sheer wealth of visual data, the painstaking chronicle of changes in dress, transport, street layouts, buildings, housing, engineering and landscape that captivates us so much today. His remarkable images offer us a powerful link with the past and with the lives of our ancestors.

THE VALUE OF THE ARCHIVE TODAY

Computers have now made it possible for Frith's many thousands of images to be accessed almost instantly. Frith's images are increasingly used as visual resources, by social historians, by researchers into genealogy and ancestry, by architects and town planners, and by teachers involved in local history projects.

In addition, the archive offers every one of us an opportunity to examine the places where we and our families have lived and worked down the years. Highly successful in Frith's own era, the archive is now, a century and more on, entering a new phase of popularity. Historians consider the Francis Frith Collection to be of prime national importance. It is the only archive of its kind remaining in private ownership. Francis Frith's archive is now housed in an historic timber barn in the beautiful village of Teffont in Wiltshire. Its founder would not recognize the archive office as it is today. In place of the many thousands of dusty boxes containing glass plate negatives and an all-pervading odour of photographic chemicals, there are now ranks of computer screens. He would be amazed to watch his images travelling round the world at unimaginable speeds through internet lines.

The archive's future is both bright and exciting. Francis Frith, with his unshakeable belief in making photographs available to the greatest number of people, would undoubtedly approve of what is being done today with his lifetime's work. His photographs depicting our shared past are now bringing pleasure and enlightenment to millions around the world a century and more after his death.

SUFFOLK
AN INTRODUCTION

THE photographs in this collection date mainly from the 1950s and 1960s. A smaller group from 1896 to 1937 focuses on churches and other prominent buildings. Included here are views of churches, chapels, houses of timber, plaster and brick from the 15th to 19th centuries, manor houses, water mills and windmills, the coastline, rivers, the Broads and the varied countryside that makes the Suffolk landscape unique.

Suffolk is bounded on the north by the River Waveney and on the south by the River Stour. The latter is renowned for its links with the artist John Constable at East Bergholt and Flatford. To the east are the coastal villages of Kessingland, Walberswick, Dunwich, Orford, Bawdsey, Walton and Shotley. There are also river estuaries here. The Blyth has to be crossed either by the bridge at Blythburgh, or by the ferry between Walberswick and Southwold. Waldringfield and Melton are on the Deben, while Trimley, Shotley,

KERSEY, *The Street c1965* K136042

Pin Mill and Woolverstone are on the Orwell.

There are about 50 miles of coastline in Suffolk, giving a varied landscape of estuary, salt marshes, heath, cliffs, sand dunes and shingle. Much of this is now protected as Heritage Coast, or as areas of Outstanding Natural Beauty. Dunwich Heath and Orford Ness are owned by the National Trust, Minsmere by the RSPB, and the Reserve at Walberswick by English Nature.

The coastal landscape features in several major literary works of the 18th and 19th centuries. The Rev George Crabbe, whose poems based on Aldeburgh later become the basis for several operas by Benjamin Britten, lived at Parham (1792-96) and Rendham (1801-06). The smugglers tale *The History of Margaret Catchpole* by the Rev Richard Cobbold includes Orford Ness, where the Excise Officers have a violent struggle with John Luff's gang of smugglers. Charles Dickens, while on a visit to Sir Samuel Morton Peto at Somerleyton Hall, came across the place name Blundeston, which became the Blunderstone of his autobiographical novel *David Copperfield* in 1850. Arthur Ransome (a descendant of the Ransomes of Ransomes & Rapiers, agricultural engineers based in Ipswich) lived at Pin Mill in Chelmondiston on the Orwell from 1934 until 1939. He moored his yacht *Nancy Blackett* at Pin Mill until Harry King's boatyard built the *Selina King* as a replacement. His novel *We Didn't Mean to go to Sea* (1937) is set here. Mrs Annie Powell, landlady of The Butt and Oyster from 1918 to 1955, was the model for the children's landlady at Alma Cottage.

In the 1950s the north-eastern part of the coast, from Corton to Dunwich, became an area of holiday camps, caravan parks and camping sites. At Kessingland the caravan park is on the cliff-top near The Sailor's Home pub. Further north at Somerleyton is a section of the Broads. Sailing and boat building are represented by the Waldringfield Sailing Club on the Deben and the boatyards at Pin Mill on the Orwell. From Shotley Gate looking across the Orwell towards Harwich and Parkstone in Essex, the lightships of Trinity House can be seen.

The oldest building in any village is the parish church, most of which were recorded in the *Domesday Book*. Some adjacent parishes, like Trimley St Martin and Trimley St Mary, had their churches in adjoining churchyards. This is more to do with geographical location than the usual tales of two brothers or sisters falling out, and wanting to build their own church.

All the churches included here have medieval origins, and were altered in the 14th or 15th century and restored in the Victorian period. Barsham has a Saxon round tower, and Bramfield a rare detached Norman round tower, while the tower at Rickinghall Inferior has been topped with a later octagonal stage with battlements. Many churches were virtually rebuilt in the 15th century, such as Blythburgh and Great Barton. Others had aisles or porches added, as at Fornham All Saints and Hitcham. Many of the photographs show churches shortly after Victorian restoration, as at Alderton and Woolverstone. At Dunwich there is a rare example of a church built on a new site in the 1830s, inland from the eroding cliffs.

The medieval and Tudor timber-framed jettied houses in Suffolk towns and villages are as much part of the landscape as the trees from which they were constructed. In the 18th century many houses were re-fronted in plaster or brick to give them a more modern appearance.

From the 1960s onwards the trend developed (now mainly halted) of exposing the whole timber framing, revealing far more than was intended by their original builders. The photographs of village streets all include timber and re-fronted timber buildings, but none of these is surpassed by the ones at Debenham, Boxford, Hartest and Cavendish and Valley Farm at Flatford.

Brick has been used as a local building material since the 15th century and very widely in the 18th and 19th centuries. Both Woolpit and Somerleyton had famous brick kilns. There are excellent examples of brick re-fronting, or houses built of brick, at Barton Mills, Brent Eleigh, Bildeston, Woolpit, Debenham, Kessingland, Kelsale, Rendham, Orford and Bawdsey.

In the 1950s and 1960s the vast majority of parishes still had a resident clergyman at the rectory or vicarage. The village school, usually dating from the Victorian period, was still open and educating successive generations of children. The village shops, including the post office, served the needs of the locals without the threat of competition from supermarkets. The village pubs, in the days before pub food, carpets and muzak, provided real ale, traditional entertainment and a sense of community.

But changes were already under way which would result in the transformation of the village community. These changes culminated in the 1960s and 1970s with the loss of railway links in the Beeching cuts after 1963; the loss of village shops, thanks to the supermarkets; the loss of village schools due to the declining child population; the loss of pubs due to the closure and amalgamation of breweries; and the loss of village crafts, as their need and use abated. Growth came to some villages in the form of new housing developments, some built by the local authority, but mainly private. The increasing population of East Anglia in general, as a place of expanding industries, second homes and retirement, also contributed to village growth.

From the 1960s onwards, the population of Suffolk rose to be one of the fastest growing areas of the British Isles. Between 1961 and 1986 the population increased by 34%, of which 90% was due to inward migration. This was stimulated by national and local planning policy, which encouraged 'London overspill' relocation to rural areas and the development of Ipswich and Felixstowe, and improved communications from the Midlands to Felixstowe Docks.

Throughout this period the impact on villages varied. Some became immersed in housing estates, with new shops, schools and social centres, while others were unaffected and continued to decline in population and lose more facilities. In the midst of this change, expansion and decline, villages or areas became conservation areas with limited growth and 'green belt'. These conserved villages became attractive to the more affluent urban middle classes as places for weekend, second or retirement homes. This has often resulted in young native villagers being unable to find, or afford, houses in their own communities.

Massive changes were also taking place in agriculture. Between 1950 and 1980 the acreage of farms increased dramatically, reducing by half the number of farms from 8,067 to 3,922. Not only holdings but fields became larger, as the era of prairie farming began, with the grubbing up of hedges. The number of combine harvesters rose from 42 in 1942 to 2,970 in 1968. These changes had a dramatic effect on the number of people employed in agriculture, which in 1981 was a mere 3.7% of the working population.

Thus in the 1950s and 1960s, when most of the photographs in this book were taken, the Suffolk village was at the end of an era. Now, for the first time, villages were no longer to be agricultural communities dependent on the land, but almost suburban communities depending on commerce, manufacturing and the growing service industries.

These photographs record every feature one would expect to find in a village: the church or chapel; the rectory or vicarage; a village green with a pump and village sign; a school; a shop; a post office; a public house, hotel or café; a garage; a village hall or reading room; a war memorial; a bus shelter; a telephone box; and a variety of houses and cottages, of different styles, dates and materials, and a manor house near the church. A view of Claydon shows a horse and trap, and at Sproughton a herd of dairy cows is on their way to the milking parlour.

In the years since these photographs were taken, the process of change has continued, with the loss of many village facilities. The church at Rickinghall Inferior was made redundant in 1977; chapels have closed in Rendham and Walberswick; schools have been closed, demolished, or changed sites as at Monks Eleigh and Bildeston; rectories and vicarages were already private houses in Bramfield and Kelsale, and have since been joined by Carlton Colville; village halls and reading rooms have closed at Sproughton, Wrentham and Old Newton; and pubs have been closed, such as at Metfield, Wrentham and Wenhaston. The majority of the shops and post offices have also ceased trading, although the post office often survives in unlikely situations – for instance, in a butcher's shop in Chelmondiston, a pub in Blythburgh and a village hall in Wenhaston. Some garages have closed, and others no longer sell petrol. These photographs almost record a lost world. They and the detailed captions certainly document the dramatic changes in rural life over the last half-century.

MILDENHALL, *Market Place c1955* M75055

13

FOREST HEATH

EXNING
The War Memorial c1955 E246005

A visitor from 1955 would be rather confused by this view (taken from the gateway of Cotton End House), as the war memorial was moved in 2001 from the centre to the right-hand side of the road and set in a new memorial garden. The late 18th-century White Horse (right) and the Victorian Grove House (centre) are virtually unchanged.

EXNING
The Church c1955
E246006

The main structure of the church and tower dates from the 14th century. Its cruciform plan with aisles and transepts is rare in Suffolk. The porch has an upper room with an external staircase. A unique double heart burial, with hands clasping the hearts, was discovered in 1971 in the south transept.

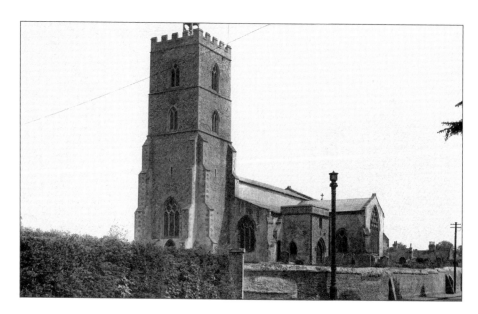

BARTON MILLS, *The Bull Inn c1965* B30005

This was a coaching inn on the London to Norwich turnpike, now the A11, since at least the mid 18th-century. The gabled red brick front dates from c1680. The side range of white brick was added in the 1920s. Two of the windows have become doors, while the grass to the left has become a car park.

MILDENHALL
West Street 1925
78282

This was renamed Queensway in 1953, to match the existing Kingsway of 1902. The manor house of the Hanmer and Bunbury families (left) was demolished in 1934-35. In the distance is the doorway of the former sweetshop on the corner of Church Lane, now Wamil Way. Behind the lime trees is The Limes, built c1800 as the town house of John Swales JP.

MILDENHALL, *Tilly's Pantry Café c1965* M75063

Situated at the top of Mill Street, Tilly's advertised '…luncheons, teas and light refreshments, everything homemade.' The building was extended to the right in 1980, and shop fronts were inserted on either side of the imposing, now central, entrance bay. The cars are an MG Magnette, a Riley Kestrel and a Ford Anglia.

MILDENHALL
Market Place c1955
M75055

The market is held on
Fridays, with the stalls
between the Victorian
pump and the 15th-century
Market Cross. Whitworth's
the grocer's is on the left-
hand corner. The Tiger's
Head, in the centre, also
had a taxi service run by Sid
Bonnett. The gabled house
was built in 1912, but it lost
its circular window when
the shop front was extended
in the 1960s.

ERISWELL
The Square c1960 E243004

On the right is a former chapel, or possibly a Quaker Meeting
House. More recently it was used by Bill Jaggard for producing
wooden decoy pigeons. Behind the willow (left of the bus shelter)
was the residence of the nurse employed by the Iveagh Estate -
the brass nameplate is still on the door. The bus shelter was built
in 1964 and cost £350. The lane leads to Little London.

ST EDMUNDSBURY

IXWORTH
High Street c1955 176003

The ancient tree was uprooted by a car in 1971. To its right is the Victorian former police station. The nearest house on the right was demolished for road widening, while the others – notice their decorated ridge tiles, Dutch gables and overhanging jetties - have been restored. Just in front of the lorry (centre) is the entrance to the Jiggins Memorial Hall, opened in 1931.

▲ IXWORTH
High Street c1955 I76022

The group of buildings on the left retain their shop fronts. The further one was J Ferguson's London House Stores, now a restaurant. The Greyhound (right) has been in the Howlett family since c1925. The wall and gateway were demolished for a car park in 1963. Beyond the telegraph pole is Ixworth Dairy.

▶ PAKENHAM
The Windmill c1960 P286004

This is the most famous of all Suffolk tower mills. Built c1820, it has been owned by the Bryant family since 1920. Two disused millstones stand either side of the doorway. To the right is a former railway carriage used as an office, while harrows and other farm machinery are assembled to the left.

▲ **GREAT BARTON**
The Main Road c1960 G338006

The traffic volume here now approaches that of
the M25. The community has obtained a crossing
and is campaigning for a bypass. The flint Post
Office Stores and cottages have changed very little;
the brickwork is still partly painted. To the left is
an entrance to Montana, a Roman Catholic
residential home.

◄ **GREAT BARTON**
The Church c1965 G338001

The tower of this large church, dating from 1441-
82, was designed by William Layer, master mason
at Bury Abbey. The turret of the aisle represented
the battlements of Jerusalem in the pre-
Reformation Palm Sunday processions. The four
new headstones, in an extension to the
churchyard, date from 1964-65.

► **CONYERS GREEN**
Livermere Road
c1960 C747009

The Vespa scooter (centre right) has just passed the turning to the Park, marked by the 18th-century Park Corner and Willow Cottages on the right. This leads into the former parkland of Great Barton Hall, sold in 1915 and gradually developed until the present day.

◄ **FORNHAM ST MARTIN**
The Church 1898
41248

The south aisle was added in 1870 in memory of the Rev E Hogg. Inside there are monuments to Sir William Gilstrap, a pottery manufacturer, of Fornham Park (who died in 1896) and Henry Claughton, an HMI in West Suffolk for 38 years (he died in 1924). Beyond are The Woolpack Inn and the Reading Room, given by the Sultan of Johore in 1886.

▲ **FORNHAM ALL SAINTS,** *The Church 1898* 41249

The 13th-century tower has rather heavy Victorian pinnacles, which were added in the 1860s. The south aisle was built after the porch. Inside, two arches of the arcade open into the nave and another one into the chancel. The parapet is inscribed 'Jesus have mercy' at the east end.

◄ **CAVENDISH**
Lower Street c1955
C509010

The Little Stores on the right now trades as Duck or Grouse, the source of many practical jokes in the village. The cinema (centre), with seating for 200, was built in 1935 by demolishing half of the old Grammar School, founded in 1696 and closed in 1907. The cinema closed in 1956. The next building was a bakery and is dated 1896. Beyond the car (centre left) is Cutting's grocers' shop.

CAVENDISH
*The Tudor Guest
House c1955* C509020

The building dates from
c1520, but it is decorated
with 20th-century
pargetting (decorative
plaster work). The Guest
House was run by the
Misses Woodward; their
advertisement
emphasised the rail link
from London via Marks
Tey to Cavendish and the
entertainment at
Cavendish Cinema.
From c1965 until 1986
this was the Grape Vine
Restaurant.

CAVENDISH, *The Church 1904* 51174

The 14th-century tower has a taller staircase with an open work bellcote. There is also a chimney from the medieval
sacristan's residence in the tower, all of which gives an unmistakable silhouette to the church. The ivy has since been
removed from the aisle, and so have the railings around the 1791 tomb of Elizabeth and William Dakings.

BABERGH

HARTEST
Cross Green c1960 H380008

Wisteria Cottage and Candlers (left) are now virtually obscured by trees. At the end of the lane, Briars had its single storey raised in 1989, with a new dormer window in the roof. West View, to the right, has tiny carved heads in the apex of the dormers. The road to the right leads down Workhouse Hill to the green.

◀ **GLEMSFORD**
Hunts Hill c1965
G235006

The telephone box on the right has gone, and the bowls green has been created behind the bungalows. The wooden British Legion Club (left) was sold in 1967; three houses were built on the site and a new Social Club was opened. In the distance are The Cock, The Angel and the Ebenezer Baptist Chapel of 1829, which closed in 1986.

28

◄ HARTEST
The Green
c1955 H380002

The village got its red telephone box (centre) listed in 1987. The former post office, called Hunter's, is to its right. The former Congregational manse is to the left, then the chapel, which closed in 1980. The shop next door was Crickmore and Savage's, a grocer's and draper's, then Osborn's, and finally Ralling's when it closed in 1990. The thatched house (left) is still Basham's, butchers since 1926.

▲ HITCHAM, *The Church c1960* H382004

This photograph was taken from outside the former Guildhall. The porch of c1470 and the battlements have flint flushwork patterns. The unusual clerestory windows were created in the 15th century by altering earlier quatrefoil windows, which remain on the less fashionable north side. The chancel was rebuilt in the 1878 restoration.

◄ NEDGING TYE
The Village c1960
N267001

'Tye' is a Suffolk and Essex term for an area of common pasture, usually called a common or a green. This view gives the impression of a large open area with houses along its boundary. Over to the left is Wattisham Air Base, famous for its air-sea rescue helicopters.

29

▶ **BILDESTON**
Aerial View c1965
B766017

This view shows the clock tower in the rectangular market place. Chapel Street and Duke Street run down towards Bildeston Hall (right). The burial ground of the Baptist chapel, rebuilt in 1844, is opposite the Hall. To the centre left is Squirrell's seed and corn merchants, now a housing development. In the distance is Wattisham Road, with 1930s Local Authority housing and the larger Brookfields Estate, begun in 1948.

◀**BILDESTON**
Market Square c1965
B766026

The clock tower was built of red and white brick in 1864. It was renovated in 1987, and has seating on the ground floor. Chandler's ironmonger's shop to the left has closed. The lean-to building has been removed to expose the overhanging jetty of the house. The growth has now been cleared off the gabled White Lodge.

▲ **BILDESTON,** *Chapel Street c1965* B766025A

The weavers' cottages (right) are reminiscent of Kersey and Lavenham. They were restored in about 1960, when seven dwellings were reduced to three. The steps of the redundant doorways were removed, but the wonderfully precarious bay window was fortunately retained. On the left is the front wall and schoolmaster's house of the Elementary School of 1853 and 1896. The grassy banks remain, but they have been straightened and tamed.

◀ **BILDESTON**
The Village c1965
B766019

On the right the large bay windows of the clock and electrical shops have been entirely removed. The fish and chip shop beyond, where it seems customers are heading, is now a hairdressers'. On the right are a series of former shop fronts in both brick and timbered buildings. In the distance is Eade's newsagent's shop and the exposed timbers of The Crown.

CHELSWORTH
All Saints' Church c1960
C746015

The church was rendered over in the early 20th century, and (controversially but correctly) colour-washed in 1993. Inside is the most magnificent tomb recess in Suffolk, dating from c1320. The porch has 15th-century figures of a lion and a griffin on the parapet. The south door is an 1843 copy of the medieval inner door. The three headstones (right) are for the Tampion family, including Thomas, the village blacksmith, who died in 1853.

CHELSWORTH, *The Bridge and The Peacock Inn c1965* C746014

The River Brett is spanned by two adjoining 18th-century hump-backed bridges, one of which is dated 1754. The Peacock (centre), named after the owner and not the bird, had a shop, which shut in 1977, built under the jetty in the 18th century. The house to the left, built c1500, had a single-storey shop extension added c1800. The house to the right has been rebuilt with dormer windows.

CHELSWORTH
The Street c1960
C746001

Because of the river and parkland on the right, most of the houses are to the left of the road. The nearer house was re-fronted in Victorian brick, and has a 17th-century chimney stack on the far wing. The cluster of gables belongs to the Old Manor and the Old Forge. The car in the distance is parked by the village hall.

CHELSWORTH, *The Village c1960* C746010

This is The Old Forge, which dates from c1500. There are two original windows with moulded mullions, and a central chimneystack with three octagonal 16th-century brick shafts. The single-storey wing was added in the 18th century. This was the forge of Thomas Tampion, whose grave we noted in the churchyard. The village hall is set back beyond the end of the building.

MONKS ELEIGH
The Green c1965
M270005

This tapering green with the church at the top is very similar to the green at Long Melford, although it is smaller. The primary school (left), built as an elementary school in 1872, was demolished in 1985. The buildings round the green date from the 18th to 19th centuries, with the exception of the 17th-century barn with a hipped and thatched roof to the right of the church. The village won the Best Kept Village Competition in 1965, hence the sign on the green.

▼ **MONKS ELEIGH,** *The Street c1965* M270002

The imposing early 19th-century building to the right is timber-framed, with the ground floor of the house imitating stone blocks; the shop front has fluted Ionic pilasters. The Post Office and Stores closed in March 2003. The lean-to is all that remains of the carpenter's and undertaker's shops. On the corner of the green is the 18th-century Swan Inn (centre right), while nearer is a pair of Victorian cottages dated 1870.

► **MONKS ELEIGH**
Swingleton c1965
M270008

To the south of Monks Eleigh's main street, and separated from it by the River Brett, is the small hamlet of Swingleton Green and Back Lane. These houses are in the latter. The nearest house is the Old Bakery; then comes Church's, a hall house of c1480, followed by a row of six artisans' cottages. To the right is the roof of the 16th-century Hobarts.

BRENT ELEIGH
The Street c1960
B615005

The street is now a cul-de-sac since the opening of the by-pass in the 1980s. The imposing red brick almshouses (right), built by Edward Colman in 1731, were modernised in 1966. Beyond Cundys Lane is High Bank, a medieval hall-house; then comes the thatched 17th-century Tudor Cottage and the former post office. On the left is the weather-boarded former water and steam mill once owned by the Beere family.

BRENT ELEIGH
Street Farm c1960
B615007

This is at the end of the village street, cut off by the bypass which nearly runs between the two 'goal posts' (left) - this idyllic view cannot be seen today. The building dates from c1480, and originally comprised a central hall and the jettied wing to the left. The central gabled window is inscribed WB1880, for Walter Brown of Brent Eleigh Hall.

**GREAT
WALDINGFIELD**
The Church 1900
45081

The west door of the
tower bears shields for
Sir Andrew and Lady
Boteler, who died in the
mid 15th century. The
rest of the church was
rebuilt in the same
period by John Appleton,
who is commemorated
in an inscription on the
south battlements. The
reason for the different
texture of the chancel is
its rebuilding in 1866-69
to the designs of William
Butterfield.

BOXFORD, *The View from the Church Tower c1965* B620027

Bridge House, the Post Office Stores and the adjoining houses (centre bottom) follow the curve of the street, named after
The Swan Inn. The shop on the right is Henry Grimwood's grocer's, run by the family from 1926 to 1989. The red brick
Ashley House, with the large white gable (centre), was built for Joseph Simpson in 1875; due to its cost, it was known as
Simpson's Folly. The white Falcon House beyond was formerly an inn.

BOXFORD
Swan Street c1955 B620004

The 18th-century brick-fronted Swan (left) closed in the 1980s.
The Victorian stepped gables, porch and Tudor-style windows of
Old Castle House beyond mask a timber building of c1600. The
adjoining Victoria Cottage with round-topped windows is dated
1839. Commerce House was Kingsbury's the builders, established
in 1730. There are several small shops on the right, one of which
has painted bands imitating beams and a panel of pargetting -
only the latter remains today.

► **BOXFORD**
Broad Street c1955
B620006

On the left is Norman's grocery and general shop, now a newsagent's. The shop front now extends half the width of the building. The shop next door with the two gables and jettied front was C J Newell's butcher's shop. The Fleece Hotel beyond, with its 18th-century front, is renowned for its jazz sessions in the upper room. The arched footbridge gives access over the River Brett, which flows through the village.

◄ **BOXFORD**
Stone Street c1955
B620012

This hamlet is to the south of Boxford and separated from it since 1975 by the bypass. This community is a Kersey in miniature, with a tiny stream, and timber-framed, plastered, jettied and gabled houses with roof lines at all angles. It even had its own pub, The Compasses, until 1989. The shop on the right, Henry Grimwood's, closed in 1983. All the houses have been restored and the barns converted. The house to the left had pargetting decoration added in 1969.

▲ **ASSINGTON,** *The Church 1907* 58916

This stands close to the site of Assington Hall, which burnt down in 1957. Parts of the outbuildings survived, including the range to the left of the church. The interior is lined with monuments to the Gurdon family dating from the 16th to 20th centuries. Since 1907 the porch windows have been blocked. The chest tomb of c1800 is for three members of the Klopfer family of Boxford and Ipswich.

◀ **KERSEY**
The Church c1955
K136028

Views of Kersey are among the best known picturesque images of Suffolk. The terrace stepping down the hill on the left is dated 1880. The pump (just visible to the right of the steps) has now been joined by a Coronation seat. On the skyline are the lych-gate, built in memory of Sidney Arthey, who died in the First World War, and the National School of 1873.

KERSEY
The Street c1965
K136042

This view typifies the unforgettable appeal of Kersey: brick, timber and plastered houses are raised to allow for the slope, with higher and higher steps to the front doors, and there is a pleasing variety of roof levels, gables and window shapes. The peace and tranquillity are broken only by the sound of Muscovy ducks on the water splash. But all this comes at a price. One of the two pubs only opens for a few hours a week, and the only remaining shop, run by the Stiffs since 1900, closed in 1992.

◄ KERSEY
The Green c1955
K136029

This photograph was taken from the village hall looking towards the Street. The man on the left is standing in front of Leys, a medieval hall-house with a jettied wing. The garden is being mown at the 15th-century Hall House (right), which has been restored and all its timber exposed. Old Drift House, beyond (c1600), has been restored since 1955 with Tudor-style windows. Inside there is a very rare timber-framed chimneystack.

◄ KERSEY
The Village from the Church c1965
K136037

We look down through the ironwork of the churchyard entrance to the water splash, and up to Stay Barn on the other side of the Brett valley. On the right, beyond the thatched cottage, is Goymer's pork butcher's shop, which closed c1950. The gardener of nearly 40 years ago would be pleased that the box bushes on the left remain today.

▲ EAST BERGHOLT, *Gaston End c1955* E247027

The elderly men discussing their roses over the garden fence at Heatherstone would find it difficult to recognise this view today. The house on the left has been replaced, while the one straight ahead is now tiled and hidden by trees. A small length of the iron fencing remains outside Heatherstone, and the gate piers opposite at Tufnells are still there. A footpath behind the men now leads to a housing estate.

◄ FLATFORD
Constable's Lane 1907 57555

This lane leads down to the Flatford Mill complex, now owned by the National Trust. The fencing rails almost seem to grow out of the trunks of the ancient oak trees, one of which at least has been pollarded. The elderly labourer is sitting on a wooden wheelbarrow, resting on his spade, with his buskins tied up with cord.

FLATFORD
*The Thatched
Cottage Tea Gardens
c1955* F31002

Boats can be hired to the left of the bridge, and tea is still served in the garden. The wooden edging along the river Stow is weathered and less defined today. The thatched Bridge House now has an eyebrow over its ground floor window. The restored dry dock of Constable's painting *Boatbuilding* (1814) is to the right of the photograph.

FLATFORD, *The Manor House c1960* F31046

This Grade I building, now called Valley Farm, is the Warden's House of the Field Studies Council, who run environmental and arts courses at Flatford Mill, Willy Lott's House and Valley Farm. It is an open hall house of c1480, with a gabled wing containing re-used 14th-century timbers. The cross passage still leads to the service rooms on the right and the hall to the left, lit by the original six-light window.

SHOTLEY GATE
The View towards Parkstone c1953
S581002

The Harwich Gas Works stands high above the horizon, left of centre. Two of the three ships are part of the reserve lightships of Trinity House based at Harwich. To the left is *Midbarrow* from the Thames Estuary, to the right *Shipwash* from the sands off Aldeburgh. In the centre is a North Sea ferry of the Steam Ship Company of Copenhagen.

CHELMONDISTON, *The Red Lion c1955* C511012

The Red Lion changed its name to The Venture (a ship) in 1997. The 1880s red brick house beyond with veranda under the gable was part of the Berners' estate at Woolverton Hall. Set back out of view is the Methodist chapel of 1879. The Post Office and Stores (centre) run by C J Brook closed in 2002. On the left, the rounded brick building is now part of Hollingsworth's butcher's shop. A sign at Inglenook shows it to have been a café; beyond is The Foresters' Arms.

PIN MILL
The Butt and Oyster
c1955 P370018

This open space was
created as a car park in 1921
by demolishing a cottage.
The single-storey extension
to the pub also dates from
1921, when Hiskey Golding
was the landlord. Where the
Austin Sevens are parked is
now a beer garden. One of
the sailing barges that used
to work the coast and the
River Orwell is laid up at the
water's edge.

▶ **PIN MILL**
*The Boatyard
1921* 70421

The maltings (centre) are a reminder of the days when grain was unloaded into the barges here en route for Ipswich. The boatyard of Harry King & Sons, 'Yacht and Boat Builders and General Repairers', is still there. Arthur Ransome included Pin Mill and its activities in *We Didn't Mean to go to Sea* (1937).

◀ **WOOLVERSTONE**
The Church c1955
W443002

The church is surrounded by the parkland of Woolverstone Hall. The exterior looks unusual because the church was rebuilt three times by the Berners family between 1830 and 1890. The porch stands against the nave of 1864, the chancel of which is black flint with stone courses. In 1888-90 a new nave and chancel were built over the north aisle of 1830, which left the earlier church as the new south aisle and chapel.

▲ **WOOLVERSTONE,** *The Village c1955* W443009

These model estate cottages were built by the Berners family for their agricultural labourers and artisans. The walled gardens were large enough to make each family self-sufficient in vegetables, thus helping to preserve their health. Most of the farm buildings survive today, except for the large barn. Beyond this group is the road to Cat House Hard on the Orwell.

◄ **SPROUGHTON**
The Wild Man c1965
S584018

This pub is named after the Woodwose, or wild man of the woods. He is usually shown as he is on the sign here - bearded, hairy and carrying a club. In the medieval period he represented good fighting evil in the form of a lion or other wild animal. Both he and the lion are carved on the shafts of fonts throughout East Anglia.

SPROUGHTON
The Mill c1955
S584001

There has been a mill on this site since Domesday. The present red brick structure dates from c1780. The wheel is an undershot wheel, and the millrace is fed through the two brick arches. The mill ceased working in 1947, and all the internal fittings and machinery have been removed. The adjacent house is of c1600, with additions up to the Victorian period.

SPROUGHTON, *The Stores c1965* S584021

Lower House (right) and the former shop date from 1520-50. The late 19th-century shop front is inserted under the jetty. The Branks family ran the shop, which shut in 1992. Rectory Cottage with its church-like doorway (left) was occupied by W Wigg, 'Sign Writer and Decorator'. The ridged roofline to the right is the Foster-Mellier Memorial and Reading Room of 1905.

SPROUGHTON, *Lower Street c1955* S584002

The herd of dairy cattle is making its way to Hall Farm, which included the former tithe barn dating from the 17th century. The parish council restored the barn in 1985 and converted it into a community and sports hall. The two gables with bargeboards (centre) belong to almshouses founded by Elizabeth Bull in 1634, rebuilt in 1876 and modernised in 1976. Beyond is the village lock-up and Cage House.

MID SUFFOLK

CLAYDON
Main Road c1955 C510001

This row of three cottages of c1630 was originally one house, which had been divided by 1823; it was restored in 1980. A new dormer was inserted over the rear window, and the gable window was blocked. The central cottage has a shop window, and it was a pick-up point for Express Parcels. At the far end is The Greyhound Inn, with the phone box opposite.

CLAYDON
*The Village from
Claydon Hill c1955*
C510005

This view was taken
from Old Ipswich Road,
now cut off by the A14.
The thatched house (left)
is The Rooks of c1620,
with a huge
chimneystack of c1800.
The horse and trap is
passing the Forge, now
closed and rebuilt.
Beyond is the garage,
also closed, and the
white gable of The
Crown Inn and Café.

OLD NEWTON, *The Shoulder of Mutton c1965* O97016

The Mutton, as it is known locally, is in the centre of the village, with the old forge to the left and the church away to the
right. To the left is Thurston's Agricultural Engineers, which began as a wheelwright's. The small building behind the finger
post was Cooper's butcher's shop (centre left). To the right is the Victorian village hall, now a house.

WOOLPIT, *The Old Mill c1960* W442030

This post mill was rebuilt in 1788 and 1844, retaining a main beam dated 1644. It was featured in an early film about milling in 1939, *And Now They Rest*. The mill was owned by the Elmer family until 1953, when it ceased working. In 1963 it was blown down in high winds, only hours before it was to be dismantled to repair Holton mill.

WOOLPIT, *The Carved Roof of St Mary's Church c1955* W442011

This is a double hammer beam roof, an exclusively East Anglian structure of which Suffolk has two-thirds of the total. There are 106 angels on the hammers, wall plate and wall posts, all with outstretched wings hovering over the congregation at worship. At the end is the Canopy of Honour, which may have been part of the original design, but which was most probably added in the 1840s.

WOOLPIT
The Post Office c1960
W442022

The post office and the two houses to the right were originally one house of c1520. The next range to the left is also 16th-century; it contains Addisons' shop, which started in 1889. Behind the tree is the arched entrance to the stable yard of the former Swan Inn, which still has a painted sign 'Ring for Ostler'.

► **WOOLPIT**
The Village c1960
W442028

This view from the church tower shows Tudor Rose Cottage of c1530, which once extended into the churchyard. On the far side of the market place is the former Swan Inn (left), with a frontage dated 1757. The double-gabled building is the Village Institute War Memorial and Museum. The notice board hides a blocked door, while the actual door has since become a window as the result of recent alterations.

◄ **BEYTON**
The Bear Inn c1955
B877008

The 19th-century front has imitation dormer windows with mock-Tudor timbers forming the top of the upstairs widows. The right-hand door is now a window. The stable block was demolished, and three houses were built as part of the Bear Close development in 1996-97. The stone by the inn sign is hollowed out as a drinking trough.

▲ **BEYTON,** *Jeavons Nursery c1955* B877006

This nursery was established in 1950. In the centre Vera, wife of Reg Jeavons the owner, is helping to pick larkspur. The house, built in 1950 and called Brooklands, remains, now surrounded by a housing development called The Garden, Field House Close and Fallowfield. The nursery business has moved, but continues to be run by Reg's nephew Ray Turner.

◄ **ELMSWELL**
The Church c1960
E171001

The battlements are under repair, hence the flat top to the tower. The tower is covered with flushwork symbols for saints, especially Mary and Edmund, and has an inscription commemorating William Maundevyl (d1503). The end of the aisle is blocked by the monument of Sir Robert Gardener (d1620), who built the almshouses behind us. The gravestone under the window, dated 1695, has skeletons holding spades, surrounded by bones.

▼ **ELMSWELL,** *The Post Office and Stores c1965* E171011

The shop (centre) was owned by W A Leeks, who had the new house (right) built in 1965. The shop traded under the same name even though it was owned by Tony Green from 1971. He sold the shop to the Stowmarket Co-op in 1975 and retained the post office. The Ipswich Co-op built a new store, which masks the right side of the buildings.

▶ **WALSHAM-LE-WILLOWS**
The Causeway c1955
W324003

The 15th-century church tower has a bull, a griffin and two lions (representing Edward IV) as pinnacles. The further gable is the Priory Room, built in 1902 by John Martineau as a Sunday school room. The central house is mainly 18th-century. Priors Close, with dormer windows, is of c1600, and has an Edwardian veranda on the front.

WALSHAM-LE-WILLOWS
The Street c1955
W324002

The Six Bells (left) dates from the 16th century, but it only became a pub in c1844; it was named The Six Bells in c1860, after the church bells to the right. The weather-boarded building (centre) was built as the Guildhall, which later became the workhouse. The next house was Clamp's General Stores. On the right is the sign of The Blue Boar.

▶ WALSHAM-LE-WILLOWS
The Street c1955
W324016

We are looking towards the church. The house on the left was the bakery of William Kenny; hidden behind the next building is the Reading Room of 1858. To the right is Harry Nunn's hardware shop, which closed in c1980. David Collins was the owner of the Post Office Stores and chemist's shop(centre right). The awning beyond is Chilliston's General Store.

WALSHAM-LE-WILLOWS
Riverside c1955
W324012

The bridge, now replaced, leads to Clarke's of Walsham, builders' merchants since 1944-45, and Bank House, where Lloyds had a branch from 1912 to 1976. On the right, the open space is part of Clarke's. The building with the classical portico (centre distance) is the Congregational chapel of 1844. To its right is a single-storey shop, Rolfe's the butcher's.

RICKINGHALL, *The Church c1955* R327005

The Norman round tower has a 15th-century octagonal top with battlements. Recent repairs have shown that there is an earlier tower beneath the outer skin of flints. The 14th-century porch was later heightened to form an upper room, hence the small low windows. The tall monument is to Lt Richard Maul (d1874). The author's in-laws, Dorothy and Harry Goddard, are buried east of the chancel. Church Farmhouse is in the distance.

RICKINGHALL
The Street c1965
R327004

The churchyard, the bus shelter of c1960 and the white house on the right are in Rickinghall Inferior, while all the rest are in Superior. The shop on the corner was the drapery and grocery store of Mrs Davey. The thatched house with the gable chimney (centre right) was the blacksmith's, although the forge was beyond the next house.

RICKINGHALL, *The Village c1965* R327008

Rickinghall Inferior is to the left of the road, with Superior to the right. The open land with the horse chestnut trees has become a housing development, although Jubilee House was built by Daniel Goddard and Sons in c1935. On the right is the butcher's shop. In the distance, above the car, is the high-class draper's and grocer's shop of Aldrich and Bryant.

BOTESDALE
The Village c1960
B619006

On the left, in Rickinghall Inferior, is the bow window of Edmund Kerry's hardware and newsagent's shop. The next house beside The Bell Hotel has been demolished. Set back before the gable of Southgate Farmhouse is the wheelwright's shop of Eric Burroughes in the former Congregational chapel. The large building across the market place was Chilver's from 1945 to 1989 - the name is retained. The war memorial is in the centre of the market place.

◄ RICKINGHALL
The Church c1965
R327003

The 14th-century tower had battlements added a century later. The nave was rebuilt at the same time - it is 30 feet wide. There is a blocked arch under the window, where a chapel has been demolished. The porch has an unusual extra buttress which here masks some of the decoration over the door. The church was restored and re-roofed in 1962, but it became redundant in 1977.

◄ BOTESDALE
The Village
c1955 B619001

We are looking from outside the 15th-century Chapel of Ease. The Angel was run by the Mason family until its closure. The group of boys (who have cycled home from either Eye Modern or Eye Grammar School) are outside Matthew's bakery, soon to be better known as Catlin's. The next but one is a grocer's, while the taller Osmond House had tearooms.

▲ **DEBENHAM,** *Cross Green c1955* D121005

The three cottages on the left were originally a house of c1580, with the further range added in c1800. When the shoemaker's single-storey, former shop beyond had been demolished, he moved into No 6. The building to the right was one house, the lower section of c1430, with the higher added in c1550. The two concrete Second World War cones (left and right) remain, the one on the left hidden in the shrubbery, the other cut into three pieces forming posts along the front fence.

◄ DEBENHAM
High Street c1955
D121009

The 16th-century house on the left still has its original brackets supporting the exposed joists of the first floor. The next house, of the same date, is at right angles to the street with a tall carriage entrance. The late 19th-century shop extension beyond is Towell's fish and chip shop. The wide 18th-century façade with seven windows is The Limes. The shop next door is Len Aldous the saddler. At the top of the hill is Bleak House, a former inn of c1540.

▼ **LAXFIELD,** *The Church c1955* L361001

The design of the tower with its faceted buttresses is very much like the one at nearby Eye. The battlements have shields representing the Wingfield and FitzLewes families, who paid for the tower in the mid 15th century. The chancel was rebuilt in a very plain style in c1820. To the right are the red brick mock-Tudor Church Villas, and to the left is the Guildhall; behind the photographer is The King's Head.

▶ **LAXFIELD**
The Street c1965
L361010

This is the broad east end of the street, with The Royal Oak of c1650 behind us, the church to the right and the Guildhall Museum of c1520 over to the left. The upstairs windows of C J Sparrow's shop are in the original house of c1580, which was extended in brick in the Victorian period. Hidden by the trees are The Villa and St Helens, originally one 18th-century house.

◄ METFIELD
The Green c1955
M269001

The former Huntsman and Hounds public house is now mostly hidden by trees. The cluster of adjacent buildings, the largest of which is the former Guildhall, are still there, and so is the pump (just visible, centre left). The railings (left) are in front of Street Farmhouse of c1600; next is The Firs, dated 1908, then Savage's shop, and in the distance the sign of The Duke William.

► METFIELD
The Village Street c1960 M269013

The group of cottages on the right, now called Honeymoon Row, have had many subsequent changes made to the roofline and dormer windows. Beyond the cycle outside Savage's shop (left) is Rose Cottage of 1904, with white busts on either side of the door. At the end is Post Office Corner.

METFIELD
Post Office Corner
c1955 M269008

The post office and shop were run by Jack Pretty, who lived in the adjoining house. The last owner was R A Boardman. The shop is now a house. Although the telephone box has gone, the post box (marked GR) has become the letterbox. From the washing on the line we can guess that it must be Monday.

METFIELD, *The Duke William c1960* M269019

Metfield once had three pubs, The Red Lion, The Huntsman and Hounds and The Duke William, of which only this one survives. The present building dates from the 1950s; it replaced an earlier beer shop with one room and a serving place. This was run by Lib Riches and Charley Borley, who became the first tenants here. Since 1960 the porch has gone, and the room to the left has been extended to twice its length.

WAVENEY

SOMERLEYTON
The Green c1955 S146008

These cottages were built by Sir Samuel Morton Peto, who made his fortune building railways in South America and East Suffolk. He owned the Somerleyton Estate from 1844 to 1861, and was responsible for the development of Lowestoft as a seaside resort. Designed by John Thomas, 28 ornamental thatched 'Tudoresque' cottages were built between 1844 and 1851 in a crescent overlooking the green. Peto's Baptist faith was the impetus for his lavish care of his estate workers.

SOMERLEYTON
The Broads c1955
S146001

This tranquil scene, with pleasure craft moored along the towpath, contrasts with the activity here in the Victorian period. The Somerleyton Brickworks, over to the left of the photograph, supplied brick via the river system both locally and nationally. Bricks from Somerleyton were used in building Liverpool Street Station in 1874.

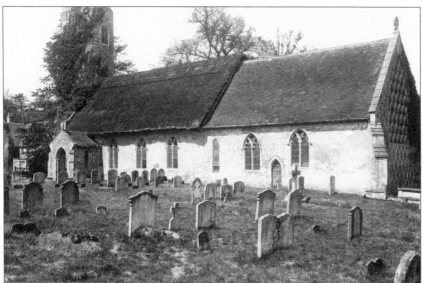

◄**BARSHAM**
The Church 1894 33351

The tower is probably Saxon, and was added to an existing nave. The east wall has diaper patterns in stonework, which continue across the window. This is possibly based on the arms of the Echingham family, patrons of the church between 1424 and 1527. The grandfather of Horatio Nelson was parson here from 1714 to 1730. His mother, Caroline Suckling, was born at the rectory to the left of the church.

SOMERLEYTON
*The School and
the Village Sign
c1955* S146005

This fantasy
building was the
village school and
master's residence,
designed by John
Thomas and built in
1848. The Crossley
family purchased
the estate in 1861,
when they
established the
custom of giving
each child a bun
and a new sixpence
every February. The
village sign,
showing a Viking
settler, was erected
in June 1949 to
celebrate the silver
wedding of Lord
and Lady
Somerleyton.

▲ **CARLTON COLVILLE,** *The Rectory c1960* C508007

This formed part of a group with the church and the Gothic village school, which are now
surrounded by housing developments. The garden and the adjacent church land was sold in the
1960s for housing. The building dates from c1600 with an 18th-century front. A Victorian Gothic
stone doorway was added later.

KESSINGLAND
High Street c1955 K137009

The hairdresser's (left), run by
Sid MacMeekin, is now unisex.
The car (a Humber) was
parked outside the Victorian
Thrift Cottages with their
round-headed doorways. The
village school was indicated by
the torch sign, beyond the car.
The garage closed in 2002, and
is being redeveloped. The bus
(right distance) was standing
outside The King's Head; it
would pass the post office and
a house dated 1864 in
ironwork on the gable, before
reaching The Queen's Head,
where the photographer was
standing.

▼ **KESSINGLAND,** *Beach Road c1955* K137024

This view is from the beach towards the village. The road was developed in the Victorian period, and most of the houses and shops, like those on the right, are of that date. On the left, 'Ivy's for Everything' has become 'Mother Hubberd's Cubberd'. The shop run by J R Smith sold a wide range of goods, including bathing costumes and caps.

► **KESSINGLAND**

The Sailor's Home c1955
K137020

There has been a pub of this name here since c1895. A single-storey extension has been added to the front, and all the chimneys and the sign have been removed. The landlord, W J Payne, could be contacted on Kessingland 245. The buildings on the right are Seaside Villas, Geneva Cottage and Jubilee Place, which are dated either 1887 or 1897.

◄ KESSINGLAND
The Beach c1955
K137032

This view looks north along the beach. The fishing boat is drawn up on the beach, and in front of the boat a child makes sandcastles in the narrow strip of pebble-free sand. The caravan site is to the left. In the middle is the Sailor's Home, with the Victorian Beach Villa to the right.

► WRENTHAM
The Church c1965
W444019

The church is to the west of the village, adjacent to the entrance to Wrentham Hall. Because of its high position, the tower was used as a government lookout and signal station in 1804, when Napoleon was expected to invade. The Celtic cross is the war memorial, erected by the Rev E R Yerburgh, on which the names are divided into Army and Navy personnel.

WRENTHAM
The Cross-Roads
c1965 W444015

The A12 runs through the
village, with Chapel Road
(leading to the
Congregational chapel of
1778) to the left and
Blythburgh Road to the
right. Wrentham Stores
(right), run by D G Sadd,
overlooks the green. The
Ford Cortina is parked
outside Broadways, an
'RAC approved tearoom
with bed and breakfast 10s
6d.' Opposite are the
Reading Room of 1888
and the village hall of
1862. A central porch was
added to Wren House, on
the left, in c1975.

SUFFOLK COASTAL

WENHASTON
The Church c1955 W440001

The small windows show the Norman origins of the church. Inside is the famous Doom painting of c1500 that once formed the background to the figures on top of the rood screen. An extra window was inserted high up to light the painting and the figures. It was whitewashed over at the Reformation, and rediscovered by accident in 1892 - it had been removed to the churchyard as rubbish – when it was taken back inside for preservation.

WENHASTON
The Street c1960
W440003

The sign of The Compasses Inn, which closed in 2001, can be seen in the distance. The double-gabled building (with the church tower just visible behind it) is the post office, which closed in 2000; since 2001 it has been situated in the village hall. Next door, St Kilda (with its brick façade) and Oakwood were originally one house built in c1600.

BRAMFIELD, *The Church c1960* B878003

This is the only church in East Anglia to have a detached Norman round tower. The rood screen still has paintings of saints, with delicate miniature hovering angels under the loft. There is a faded wall painting of the Holy Rood on the north wall. The gravestone of Bridget Applewhaite records how she died in 1737, having been 'thunderstruck' on the eve of her second marriage.

▼ **BRAMFIELD,** *The Street c1955* B878001

The Queen's Head (left) dates from c1580. It was renovated in 1982-83 when the gents' loos were removed from the car park. The roof of the former vicarage can be seen between the pub and the bus shelter of c1953. On the left is the garden of Thomas Neale's almshouses of 1723, demolished in 1968. The white gable (centre right) is the former Swan, closed in the 1930s. The adjacent village shop closed in 2001. The garage remains, on the site of the earlier smithy, but without its pumps since 1995.

▶ **BLYTHBURGH**
The Village c1955
B125004

The shop and post office, looking like a turnpike house, stands on the corner of Chapel Lane and the A12, with its sheltered entrance towards the village. It had been in the Ade family since the early 1920s until its closure in 1999. The exterior has since been rendered, masking the original flint structure.

◄ BLYTHBURGH
The Church 1891
28357

The tower dates from c1330, but the rest of the church was rebuilt c1420-1460. This is one of the largest and grandest churches in Suffolk. Imagine how the skyline would have looked with 34 statues of saints on the plinths between the clerestory windows of the nave. The church is known locally as the 'Cathedral of the Marshes'.

► WALBERSWICK
The Village Street c1955 W7026

The foundation stone of the chapel (left) was laid in 1910. The end of the next house is made up of alternate courses of brick and beach pebbles. Further on is a row of Victorian terraced cottages, with dormer and bay windows. On the right, the parked cars wait for petrol or repairs at Fisher's garage with its Esso sign.

WALBERSWICK
The Ferry c1955 W7032

The Victorian chain ferry was replaced by a steam ferry, which sank in 1942. The service was revived with a rowing boat after the Second World War. Here the postman with his cycle waits for passengers to disembark so he can deliver mail in Walberswick - a routine which continued into the 1980s. The boatman was Bob Cross, who only handed over to his nephew David Church in 1991.

◄ **WALBERSWICK**
The Green W7007

The road ahead leads to the mud flats and the ferry. Out of view to the left are a group of gift shops, established in a former house, garage and WI Hall. The single-storey building (right) was the Estate Office. The large thatched house beside it, Greenways, was built in 1930. Where the swing stands, in front of the white house (left), is now a children's play area.

◄ WALBERSWICK
The Street c1955
W7004

The first of this row of Victorian cottages has the original name, Fern Cottage, painted on the glass fanlight. An ice-cream tricycle stands outside Row End (centre). The weather-boarded hut has had a variety of uses as a sweet, craft and gift shop. It is about to be demolished and a house built on the site. In the distance a lorry heads for the village, with more ease than today.

▲ **WALBERSWICK,** *The Heronry c1955* W7025

The Southwold narrow-gauge railway ran from 1877 until 1929 with stations at Halesworth, Wenhaston, Blythburgh, Walberswick and Southwold. The route ran through this area of marsh and woodland known as the Heronry. With the relaxed timetable of the Southwold line, there was ample opportunity for poaching en route. Walter Day, a plateman, was prosecuted in 1884 for setting snares and taking hares.

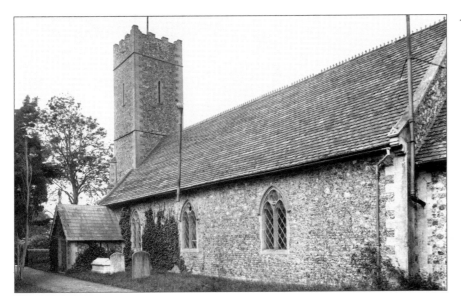

◄ DUNWICH
St James' Church 1909 62047

St James' church was named after the medieval leper hospital, whose Norman ruins lie to the east. The church was built well inland in 1830. It all looks new because the chancel was rebuilt and all the windows replaced in 1881. Just to the left of the photograph is a buttress from All Saints' church, moved here from the cliff edge in 1923.

WESTLETON, *The Village Sign c1965* W441020

Situated at the northern top of the green is the metal sign, showing a tower mill. It was erected by the Westleton Carnival Committee in 1963. The shaft and the millstone came from the mill, which was demolished the same year. The other mill had already been converted into a house by 1961.

WESTLETON
The Village c1960
W441010

The man and dog are leaving E M Caine's grocer's and newsagent's shop, which has his initials in the gable. Beyond, in the white doubled-gabled house, there is a teashop; next is the Primitive Methodist chapel of 1868, now a bookshop. The shop to the left hides The Crown Inn, where Henry James called in August 1897. Hiller's garage is in the distance.

WESTLETON, *The Church c1960* W441018

The tower fell in 1770 and has been replaced by a brick bellcote. Near the priest's door is a monument for the Rev John Hall and his wife Emily, who were with the Church Missionary Society in Palestine for 26 years. He was vicar here for 14 years; she died in 1920, he in 1921. Side by side lie two Westleton war casualties, Private Jonathan Cracknell, aged 18, who died in 1918, and Pilot A Clouting, aged 20, who died in 1942.

WESTLETON
The Village c1965
W441013

At the south end of the street is a small green, with the 1964 Best Kept Village sign. On the right is Reddish, the contractors, whose van (far left) advertises 'tile and mole draining'. In the centre is Hiller's Garage, now Scarlett, with the skeleton framework of the present workshop, which will block the view of the church from here.

▼ **YOXFORD,** *The Church 1909* 62053

It is rare in Suffolk to find a spire before the Victorian period. This one is 17th-century. The window of the Cockfield chapel is blocked by later monuments. The railed tomb (centre) is that of John Barnes (d1845). The white headstone to the left had only been erected in the previous year. It is for Ezra Cotton (d1898) and his widow Lucy (d1908).

▶ **YOXFORD**
The Griffin c1955
Y16008

The Griffin (left) is virtually unchanged, with the Victorian mock façade masking the original 17th-century timber building. The third house along, with the couple and car outside, has a delicate ironwork veranda over a classical porch. Outside is an early 19th-century milestone, inscribed 'From London 93 miles, to Hevingham Hall 5'.

◄ **YOXFORD**
High Street c1965
Y16053

The post office (left), now Minsmere House, has a façade which can be dated to 1801-02 from the insurance fire mark. On the far right is Tew & Sons' stores. A lady peers out of her shop next door, which is now Coach House Cottage. The Blois Arms (centre right) is named after the family who held the manor of Cockfield Hall from 1694.

► **KELSALE**
*Court
Convalescent
Home c1955*
K138001

This splendid early 19th-century house is the former rectory. The symmetrical front has five window bays; the central bay over the porch has rounded tops. The porch has Doric fluted columns and pilasters; the window above is recessed with shutters. The side walls have several painted dummy windows.

RENDHAM
The Church c1960
R326001

The main entrance is from the north porch, which is unusual, while the south door is blocked. Inside there is a pulpit with sounding board dated 1632, a set of 26 Victorian box pews, and an east window in memory of an aunt of Nurse Edith Cavell. Beyond is the Victorian South View Cottage, and further left is The White Horse.

RENDHAM, *The Village c1960* R326003

On the left is the site of the former red brick Independent chapel, built in 1750 and enlarged in 1834. The upper windows give light into the gallery, which faces the tall pulpit on three sides. The single-storey Sunday School and vestry are late Victorian. The chapel closed in 1979. Further on are the Victorian Wallnook Cottage and the 18th-century thatched Oakdene.

SAXSTEAD, *The Mill c1955* S578004

This post mill is one of Suffolk's best-known tourist attractions. The brick round house and wooden mill date from 1796, with Victorian alterations. The mill ceased working in 1947, but the machinery is complete and in working order. There are two pairs of stones in the buck and two pairs and a centrifugal dressing machine in the round house.

◄ **PARHAM**
The Village c1955
P339003

Church Farm (right) of c1480 is a hall house with cross wings. The parlour wing is double jettied, with the arms of the de Ufford family, Earls of Suffolk, under the oriel window. The farm was part of the Parham estate until 1921. Beyond the barns are two 17th-century groups of houses: Street Cottages and the flint and brick White Gates.

◄ **PEASENHALL**
The Village
c1960 P287001

George Horner's grocer's shop (right) has become an art gallery, and the pumps have gone from the garage. The village shop beyond remains, and so does Emmett's grocer's and draper's at the far white gable. The shop was established in c1900 and was by appointment to HM the Queen Mother purveyors of sweet pickle and mild cured ham and bacon.

▲ **UFFORD,** *The Church and Stocks 1894* 33990

Before the establishment of county police forces in the 1840s, parish constables had to punish offenders. They could either be placed in the stocks for a period of time, or whipped. Note how the whipping post has three arm positions, according to the height of the offender.

◄ **MELTON**
The Asylum 1896
37324

The central building was the Loes and Wilford House of Industry, established in 1767. It was taken over to become the County Asylum in 1829, which was enlarged over the years and closed in April 1993, when it was called St Audrey's Hospital. Dr John Kirkman was the medical officer from 1831 to 1875. During this time he pioneered occupational therapy and non-restraint in his treatments.

MELTON
The Street c1965
M268015

This shop was run by two generations of Ben Friars from around 1910 to 1982. It had its own abattoir, smoke house and mobile shop. Further on is another former shop with a chewing-gum machine; beyond it are the telephone box and the Parish Room of 1904. On the left, the low railings belong to the Engineering Works, now Thurlow, Nunn & Standen.

MELTON
*The Horse and
Groom c1955*
M268002

The left wing was added to the 18th-century front, which has an elliptical arched entrance in the central bay. The Cobbold advertising has been removed. Notice the sign on the front of the pub pointing to RAF Bentwaters, which has now closed. Skoulding's high-class provisions shop is on the right-hand corner – the road leads to the station.

BUTLEY, *The Street c1953* B618002

The lady with the pram, near the clipped bushes (left), is outside the Post Office and Stores, which closed in 1975, although the post box remains. The tall block beyond has an industrial appearance, but in fact it consists of five cottages. The barns belonged to William 'Wiggie' Large, builder and wheelwright, who lived in the adjoining house.

ORFORD
The Castle 1937
88245

This was built between 1165 and 1173 by Henry II to defend the Suffolk coast, and probably to curb the power of the Bigods of Framlingham. To improve the sight-line of the defenders and to prevent the danger of undermining, this revolutionary design had 18 faceted sides, instead of the usual four-square keep.

ORFORD, *Yachting at the Quay c1960* O20095

This assault craft-type ferry belonged to the Atomic Weapons Research Establishment at Orford Ness, 1959-71. Here they designed and tested triggering devices for the British nuclear bomb, using conventional explosives and centrifugal testing methods. In 1993 the National Trust purchased the 1500-acre site, which was opened to the public in 1995.

ORFORD
The Road to the Quay
c1965 O20102

This row of 18th-century timber-framed cottages had a red brick façade added in c1820. The shop has now shut, and its frontage has been replaced to blend in with the rest. Beyond is the gable of a builder's yard, now a dwelling. The further row has been restored, and an extension with a garage has been added so as to be almost unnoticeable.

ORFORD
Church Street c1960 O20081

We are looking east from the Market Square; the battlements of
the church can be seen to the left of Church House (extreme left).
The early 19th-century post office building with its dummy upper
window (right) closed in 1998, and the post office was relocated
in Orford Supply Stores opposite. On the corner of Quay Road is
Corner House of c1800 with black advertising panels (centre),
now gone, alas.

ALDERTON
The Church c1955
A342003

The tower was struck by lightning in 1767. It was repaired, but half of it fell during Sunday service in 1821. The only casualty was a cow grazing in the churchyard. The church was in quite a ruinous condition for 40 years, until the chancel, vestry and south wall of the nave were rebuilt in 1865.

ALDERTON, *The Swan Inn c1965* A342015

The antiquarian David Davy, who stayed here in 1830, recorded that 'finding we could be very decently taken care of here, we engaged beds, ordered a fire while our hostess was preparing us a mutton chop'. The pub was threatened with closure in 1995, but it was saved following a successful campaign to 'Save our Swan'. The car is an Austin A40.

▶ **BAWDSEY**
The Manor 1899
43242

Standing at the mouth of the River Deben, this opulent mansion was built by Sir Cuthbert Quilter in five stages between 1886 and 1904. This accounts for the impression that two different houses have been joined together. On the terrace is the newly built teahouse, with a copper dome. The arch at the bottom of the terrace is a sheltered seating area.

◀ **MARTLESHAM**
The Red Lion 1890
37325

The original timber building, dating from c1580, has two gables; the brick extension to the right is 19th-century. The (now) central gable has a delicate oriel over a wider bay window on the ground floor. The Red Lion's ship figurehead is often wrongly said to have come from a Dutch ship which fought at the battle of Sole Bay in 1672, but it actually dates from c1740. In 1896 Herbert Fletch was the landlord and local builder.

▲ **WALDRINGFIELD,** *Mill Road c1965* W438040

This photograph was taken from the church tower looking north towards the main street. The post mill, which stood to the north of the cottage, was built in 1829 and demolished in 1912. Mill Cottage and the converted barn called Granary House are all that remain of the mill complex. On the horizon is the street, mostly built up since the 1920s, but including the school of 1874.

◄**WALDRINGFIELD**
The River c1955
W438017

This is the River Deben, viewed from near the Sailing Club House looking downstream towards White House; Waldringfield is to the right and Petistree Hall, in Sutton, is over to the left. The stretch of river beyond the mud bank leads to Stanner Point, also in Sutton. In contrast to its earlier days, when the Deben was a highway of commerce, the river is now used by yachts and pleasure craft.

TRIMLEY
High Street c1960
T80008

St Mary's church, here without a tower, became a church centre in the late 1980s. The post office and adjoining house remain, but there have been many changes since 1960. The next building has been demolished, and so has the whole of the right side of the street. By the Craven A advertisement (right) we can just see a French gun barrel, which gives its name to Gun Lane, leading to Grimstone Hall.

TRIMLEY, *Mill Lane c1955* T80005

This is taken from Old Kirton Road, looking towards the capped top of the mill, now Mill Close. The cottages are Victorian and Edwardian, and some of them may have been built for workers at the kiln. Hazel Cottage, on the left, is dated 1901, and Maylea Cottage (opposite) is of the same period.

TRIMLEY
Spriteshall Lane
c1960 T80010

The water tower (rising above the house roof, right) was built in 1929 to store water for the Trimley and Walton area. It became obsolete in 2002, but it will not be demolished because of its value as a site for mobile phone masts. Slight changes since c1960 have been made to Sprites Cottage on the corner (left). The road is still unadopted, with an uneven surface.

BUCKLESHAM, *Levington Lane c1960* B616006

In the post-war period the provision of Local Authority housing increased to meet the demands of a rising population. Here we see pairs of family homes with large front and back gardens built in the late 1950s. Beyond are bungalows for the elderly, built in 1961. The hedge against the road has now grown up, almost hiding the concrete footpath from view.

WALTON
The Parish Church 1901 46695

The church looks in a pristine condition in this photograph,
which is hardly surprising, as the aisle and vestry were built in
1860 and the tower in 1899. The chancel is medieval, and its
darker surface is due to the use of brown septaria stone. To the
right now stands the former market cross, moved from Cage Lane
to Chiswick. It was returned here in 1957 when the Parish Council
converted it into a bus shelter.

INDEX

Frith Book Co Titles

www.francisfrith.co.uk

The Frith Book Company publishes over 100 new titles each year. A selection of those currently available is listed below. For latest catalogue please contact Frith Book Co.

Town Books 96 pages, approximately 100 photos. **County and Themed Books** 128 pages, approximately 150 photos (unless specified). All titles hardback with laminated case and jacket, except those indicated pb (paperback)

Amersham, Chesham & Rickmansworth (pb)	1-85937-340-2	£9.99	Devon (pb)	1-85937-297-x	£9.99
Andover (pb)	1-85937-292-9	£9.99	Devon Churches (pb)	1-85937-250-3	£9.99
Aylesbury (pb)	1-85937-227-9	£9.99	Dorchester (pb)	1-85937-307-0	£9.99
Barnstaple (pb)	1-85937-300-3	£9.99	Dorset (pb)	1-85937-269-4	£9.99
Basildon Living Memories (pb)	1-85937-515-4	£9.99	Dorset Coast (pb)	1-85937-299-6	£9.99
Bath (pb)	1-85937-419-0	£9.99	Dorset Living Memories (pb)	1-85937-584-7	£9.99
Bedford (pb)	1-85937-205-8	£9.99	Down the Severn (pb)	1-85937-560-x	£9.99
Bedfordshire Living Memories	1-85937-513-8	£14.99	Down The Thames (pb)	1-85937-278-3	£9.99
Belfast (pb)	1-85937-303-8	£9.99	Down the Trent	1-85937-311-9	£14.99
Berkshire (pb)	1-85937-191-4	£9.99	East Anglia (pb)	1-85937-265-1	£9.99
Berkshire Churches	1-85937-170-1	£17.99	East Grinstead (pb)	1-85937-138-8	£9.99
Berkshire Living Memories	1-85937-332-1	£14.99	East London	1-85937-080-2	£14.99
Black Country	1-85937-497-2	£12.99	East Sussex (pb)	1-85937-606-1	£9.99
Blackpool (pb)	1-85937-393-3	£9.99	Eastbourne (pb)	1-85937-399-2	£9.99
Bognor Regis (pb)	1-85937-431-x	£9.99	Edinburgh (pb)	1-85937-193-0	£8.99
Bournemouth (pb)	1-85937-545-6	£9.99	England In The 1880s	1-85937-331-3	£17.99
Bradford (pb)	1-85937-204-x	£9.99	Essex - Second Selection	1-85937-456-5	£14.99
Bridgend (pb)	1-85937-386-0	£7.99	Essex (pb)	1-85937-270-8	£9.99
Bridgwater (pb)	1-85937-305-4	£9.99	Essex Coast	1-85937-342-9	£14.99
Bridport (pb)	1-85937-327-5	£9.99	Essex Living Memories	1-85937-490-5	£14.99
Brighton (pb)	1-85937-192-2	£8.99	Exeter	1-85937-539-1	£9.99
Bristol (pb)	1-85937-264-3	£9.99	Exmoor (pb)	1-85937-608-8	£9.99
British Life A Century Ago (pb)	1-85937-213-9	£9.99	Falmouth (pb)	1-85937-594-4	£9.99
Buckinghamshire (pb)	1-85937-200-7	£9.99	Folkestone (pb)	1-85937-124-8	£9.99
Camberley (pb)	1-85937-222-8	£9.99	Frome (pb)	1-85937-317-8	£9.99
Cambridge (pb)	1-85937-422-0	£9.99	Glamorgan	1-85937-488-3	£14.99
Cambridgeshire (pb)	1-85937-420-4	£9.99	Glasgow (pb)	1-85937-190-6	£9.99
Cambridgeshire Villages	1-85937-523-5	£14.99	Glastonbury (pb)	1-85937-338-0	£7.99
Canals And Waterways (pb)	1-85937-291-0	£9.99	Gloucester (pb)	1-85937-232-5	£9.99
Canterbury Cathedral (pb)	1-85937-179-5	£9.99	Gloucestershire (pb)	1-85937-561-8	£9.99
Cardiff (pb)	1-85937-093-4	£9.99	Great Yarmouth (pb)	1-85937-426-3	£9.99
Carmarthenshire (pb)	1-85937-604-5	£9.99	Greater Manchester (pb)	1-85937-266-x	£9.99
Chelmsford (pb)	1-85937-310-0	£9.99	Guildford (pb)	1-85937-410-7	£9.99
Cheltenham (pb)	1-85937-095-0	£9.99	Hampshire (pb)	1-85937-279-1	£9.99
Cheshire (pb)	1-85937-271-6	£9.99	Harrogate (pb)	1-85937-423-9	£9.99
Chester (pb)	1-85937-382 8	£9.99	Hastings and Bexhill (pb)	1-85937-131-0	£9.99
Chesterfield (pb)	1-85937-378-x	£9.99	Heart of Lancashire (pb)	1-85937-197-3	£9.99
Chichester (pb)	1-85937-228-7	£9.99	Helston (pb)	1-85937-214-7	£9.99
Churches of East Cornwall (pb)	1-85937-249-x	£9.99	Hereford (pb)	1-85937-175-2	£9.99
Churches of Hampshire (pb)	1-85937-207-4	£9.99	Herefordshire (pb)	1-85937-567-7	£9.99
Cinque Ports & Two Ancient Towns	1-85937-492-1	£14.99	Herefordshire Living Memories	1-85937-514-6	£14.99
Colchester (pb)	1-85937-188-4	£8.99	Hertfordshire (pb)	1-85937-247-3	£9.99
Cornwall (pb)	1-85937-229-5	£9.99	Horsham (pb)	1-85937-432-8	£9.99
Cornwall Living Memories	1-85937-248-1	£14.99	Humberside (pb)	1-85937-605-3	£9.99
Cotswolds (pb)	1-85937-230-9	£9.99	Hythe, Romney Marsh, Ashford (pb)	1-85937-256-2	£9.99
Cotswolds Living Memories	1-85937-255-4	£14.99	Ipswich (pb)	1-85937-424-7	£9.99
County Durham (pb)	1-85937-398-4	£9.99	Isle of Man (pb)	1-85937-268-6	£9.99
Croydon Living Memories (pb)	1-85937-162-0	£9.99	Isle of Wight (pb)	1-85937-429-8	£9.99
Cumbria (pb)	1-85937-621-5	£9.99	Isle of Wight Living Memories	1-85937-304-6	£14.99
Derby (pb)	1-85937-367-4	£9.99	Kent (pb)	1-85937-189-2	£9.99
Derbyshire (pb)	1-85937-196-5	£9.99	Kent Living Memories(pb)	1-85937-401-8	£9.99
Derbyshire Living Memories	1-85937-330-5	£14.99	Kings Lynn (pb)	1-85937-334-8	£9.99

Available from your local bookshop or from the publisher

Frith Book Co Titles (continued)

Title	ISBN	Price	Title	ISBN	Price
Lake District (pb)	1-85937-275-9	£9.99	Sherborne (pb)	1-85937-301-1	£9.99
Lancashire Living Memories	1-85937-335-6	£14.99	Shrewsbury (pb)	1-85937-325-9	£9.99
Lancaster, Morecambe, Heysham (pb)	1-85937-233-3	£9.99	Shropshire (pb)	1-85937-326-7	£9.99
Leeds (pb)	1-85937-202-3	£9.99	Shropshire Living Memories	1-85937-643-6	£14.99
Leicester (pb)	1-85937-381-x	£9.99	Somerset	1-85937-153-1	£14.99
Leicestershire & Rutland Living Memories	1-85937-500-6	£12.99	South Devon Coast	1-85937-107-8	£14.99
Leicestershire (pb)	1-85937-185-x	£9.99	South Devon Living Memories (pb)	1-85937-609-6	£9.99
Lighthouses	1-85937-257-0	£9.99	South East London (pb)	1-85937-263-5	£9.99
Lincoln (pb)	1-85937-380-1	£9.99	South Somerset	1-85937-318-6	£14.99
Lincolnshire (pb)	1-85937-433-6	£9.99	South Wales	1-85937-519-7	£14.99
Liverpool and Merseyside (pb)	1-85937-234-1	£9.99	Southampton (pb)	1-85937-427-1	£9.99
London (pb)	1-85937-183-3	£9.99	Southend (pb)	1-85937-313-5	£9.99
London Living Memories	1-85937-454-9	£14.99	Southport (pb)	1-85937-425-5	£9.99
Ludlow (pb)	1-85937-176-0	£9.99	St Albans (pb)	1-85937-341-0	£9.99
Luton (pb)	1-85937-235-x	£9.99	St Ives (pb)	1-85937-415-8	£9.99
Maidenhead (pb)	1-85937-339-9	£9.99	Stafford Living Memories (pb)	1-85937-503-0	£9.99
Maidstone (pb)	1-85937-391-7	£9.99	Staffordshire (pb)	1-85937-308-9	£9.99
Manchester (pb)	1-85937-198-1	£9.99	Stourbridge (pb)	1-85937-530-8	£9.99
Marlborough (pb)	1-85937-336-4	£9.99	Stratford upon Avon (pb)	1-85937-388-7	£9.99
Middlesex	1-85937-158-2	£14.99	Suffolk (pb)	1-85937-221-x	£9.99
Monmouthshire	1-85937-532-4	£14.99	Suffolk Coast (pb)	1-85937-610-x	£9.99
New Forest (pb)	1-85937-390-9	£9.99	Surrey (pb)	1-85937-240-6	£9.99
Newark (pb)	1-85937-366-6	£9.99	Surrey Living Memories	1-85937-328-3	£14.99
Newport, Wales (pb)	1-85937-258-9	£9.99	Sussex (pb)	1-85937-184-1	£9.99
Newquay (pb)	1-85937-421-2	£9.99	Sutton (pb)	1-85937-337-2	£9.99
Norfolk (pb)	1-85937-195-7	£9.99	Swansea (pb)	1-85937-167-1	£9.99
Norfolk Broads	1-85937-486-7	£14.99	Taunton (pb)	1-85937-314-3	£9.99
Norfolk Living Memories (pb)	1-85937-402-6	£9.99	Tees Valley & Cleveland (pb)	1-85937-623-1	£9.99
North Buckinghamshire	1-85937-626-6	£14.99	Teignmouth (pb)	1-85937-370-4	£7.99
North Devon Living Memories	1-85937-261-9	£14.99	Thanet (pb)	1-85937-116-7	£9.99
North Hertfordshire	1-85937-547-2	£14.99	Tiverton (pb)	1-85937-178-7	£9.99
North London (pb)	1-85937-403-4	£9.99	Torbay (pb)	1-85937-597-9	£9.99
North Somerset	1-85937-302-x	£14.99	Truro (pb)	1-85937-598-7	£9.99
North Wales (pb)	1-85937-298-8	£9.99	Victorian & Edwardian Dorset	1-85937-254-6	£14.99
North Yorkshire (pb)	1-85937-236-8	£9.99	Victorian & Edwardian Kent (pb)	1-85937-624-X	£9.99
Northamptonshire Living Memories	1-85937-529-4	£14.99	Victorian & Edwardian Maritime Album (pb)	1-85937-622-3	£9.99
Northamptonshire	1-85937-150-7	£14.99	Victorian and Edwardian Sussex (pb)	1-85937-625-8	£9.99
Northumberland Tyne & Wear (pb)	1-85937-281-3	£9.99	Villages of Devon (pb)	1-85937-293-7	£9.99
Northumberland	1-85937-522-7	£14.99	Villages of Kent (pb)	1-85937-294-5	£9.99
Norwich (pb)	1-85937-194-9	£8.99	Villages of Sussex (pb)	1-85937-295-3	£9.99
Nottingham (pb)	1-85937-324-0	£9.99	Warrington (pb)	1-85937-507-3	£9.99
Nottinghamshire (pb)	1-85937-187-6	£9.99	Warwick (pb)	1-85937-518-9	£9.99
Oxford (pb)	1-85937-411-5	£9.99	Warwickshire (pb)	1-85937-203-1	£9.99
Oxfordshire (pb)	1-85937-430-1	£9.99	Welsh Castles (pb)	1-85937-322-4	£9.99
Oxfordshire Living Memories	1-85937-525-1	£14.99	West Midlands (pb)	1-85937-289-9	£9.99
Paignton (pb)	1-85937-374-7	£7.99	West Sussex (pb)	1-85937-607-x	£9.99
Peak District (pb)	1-85937-280-5	£9.99	West Yorkshire (pb)	1-85937-201-5	£9.99
Pembrokeshire	1-85937-262-7	£14.99	Weston Super Mare (pb)	1-85937-306-2	£9.99
Penzance (pb)	1-85937-595-2	£9.99	Weymouth (pb)	1-85937-209-0	£9.99
Peterborough (pb)	1-85937-219-8	£9.99	Wiltshire (pb)	1-85937-277-5	£9.99
Picturesque Harbours	1-85937-208-2	£14.99	Wiltshire Churches (pb)	1-85937-171-x	£9.99
Piers	1-85937-237-6	£17.99	Wiltshire Living Memories (pb)	1-85937-396-8	£9.99
Plymouth (pb)	1-85937-389-5	£9.99	Winchester (pb)	1-85937-428-x	£9.99
Poole & Sandbanks (pb)	1-85937-251-1	£9.99	Windsor (pb)	1-85937-333-x	£9.99
Preston (pb)	1-85937-212-0	£9.99	Wokingham & Bracknell (pb)	1-85937-329-1	£9.99
Reading (pb)	1-85937-238-4	£9.99	Woodbridge (pb)	1-85937-498-0	£9.99
Redhill to Reigate (pb)	1-85937-596-0	£9.99	Worcester (pb)	1-85937-165-5	£9.99
Ringwood (pb)	1-85937-384-4	£7.99	Worcestershire Living Memories	1-85937-489-1	£14.99
Romford (pb)	1-85937-319-4	£9.99	Worcestershire	1-85937-152-3	£14.99
Royal Tunbridge Wells (pb)	1-85937-504-9	£9.99	York (pb)	1-85937-199-x	£9.99
Salisbury (pb)	1-85937-239-2	£9.99	Yorkshire (pb)	1-85937-186-8	£9.99
Scarborough (pb)	1-85937-379-8	£9.99	Yorkshire Coastal Memories	1-85937-506-5	£14.99
Sevenoaks and Tonbridge (pb)	1-85937-392-5	£9.99	Yorkshire Dales	1-85937-502-2	£14.99
Sheffield & South Yorks (pb)	1-85937-267-8	£9.99	Yorkshire Living Memories (pb)	1-85937-397-6	£9.99

See Frith books on the internet at www.francisfrith.co.uk

FRITH PRODUCTS & SERVICES

Francis Frith would doubtless be pleased to know that the pioneering publishing venture he started in 1860 still continues today. Over a hundred and forty years later, The Francis Frith Collection continues in the same innovative tradition and is now one of the foremost publishers of vintage photographs in the world. Some of the current activities include:

Interior Decoration

Today Frith's photographs can be seen framed and as giant wall murals in thousands of pubs, restaurants, hotels, banks, retail stores and other public buildings throughout the country. In every case they enhance the unique local atmosphere of the places they depict and provide reminders of gentler days in an increasingly busy and frenetic world.

Product Promotions

Frith products are used by many major companies to promote the sales of their own products or to reinforce their own history and heritage. Frith promotions have been used by Hovis bread, Courage beers, Scots Porage Oats, Colman's mustard, Cadbury's foods, Mellow Birds coffee, Dunhill pipe tobacco, Guinness, and Bulmer's Cider.

Genealogy and Family History

As the interest in family history and roots grows world-wide, more and more people are turning to Frith's photographs of Great Britain for images of the towns, villages and streets where their ancestors lived; and, of course, photographs of the churches and chapels where their ancestors were christened, married and buried are an essential part of every genealogy tree and family album.

Frith Products

All Frith photographs are available Framed or just as Mounted Prints and Posters (size 23 x 16 inches). These may be ordered from the address below. From time to time other products - Address Books, Calendars, Table Mats, etc - are available.

The Internet

Already fifty thousand Frith photographs can be viewed and purchased on the internet through the Frith websites and a myriad of partner sites.

For more detailed information on Frith companies and products, look at these sites:

www.francisfrith.co.uk
www.francisfrith.com
(for North American visitors)

See the complete list of Frith Books at:

www.francisfrith.co.uk

This web site is regularly updated with the latest list of publications from the Frith Book Company. If you wish to buy books relating to another part of the country that your local bookshop does not stock, you may purchase on-line.

For further information, trade, or author enquiries please contact us at the address below:
The Francis Frith Collection, Frith's Barn, Teffont, Salisbury, Wiltshire, England SP3 5QP.
Tel: +44 (0)1722 716 376 Fax: +44 (0)1722 716 881 Email: sales@francisfrith.co.uk

---

See Frith books on the internet at www.francisfrith.co.uk

FREE MOUNTED PRINT

Mounted Print
Overall size 14 x 11 inches

Fill in and cut out this voucher and return
it with your remittance for £2.25 (to cover postage and handling). Offer valid for delivery to UK addresses only.

Choose any photograph included in this book.
Your SEPIA print will be A4 in size. It will be mounted in a cream mount with a burgundy rule line (overall size 14 x 11 inches).

Order additional Mounted Prints at HALF PRICE (only £7.49 each*)
If you would like to order more Frith prints from this book, possibly as gifts for friends and family, you can buy them at half price (with no additional postage and handling costs).

Have your Mounted Prints framed
For an extra £14.95 per print* you can have your mounted print(s) framed in an elegant polished wood and gilt moulding, overall size 16 x 13 inches (no additional postage and handling required).

---

* IMPORTANT!

These special prices are only available if you order at the same time as you order your free mounted print. You must use the ORIGINAL VOUCHER on this page (no copies permitted). We can only despatch to one address.

Send completed Voucher form to:
The Francis Frith Collection, Frith's Barn, Teffont, Salisbury, Wiltshire SP3 5QP

Voucher for *FREE* and Reduced Price Frith Prints

Please do not photocopy this voucher. Only the original is valid, so please fill it in, cut it out and return it to us with your order.

Picture ref no	Page no	Qty	Mounted @ £7.49	Framed + £14.95	Total Cost
		1	Free of charge*	£	£
			£7.49	£	£
			£7.49	£	£
			£7.49	£	£
			£7.49	£	£
			£7.49	£	£
Please allow 28 days for delivery			* Post & handling (UK)		£2.25
			Total Order Cost		£

Title of this book . . . .

I enclose a cheque/postal order for £ . . . .
made payable to 'The Francis Frith Collection'

OR please debit my Mastercard / Visa / Switch / Amex card
(credit cards please on all overseas orders), details below

Card Number

Issue No (Switch only)   Valid from (Amex/Switch)

Expires   Signature

Name Mr/Mrs/Ms . . . .

Address . . . .

. . . .

. . . .

. . . . Postcode . . . .

Daytime Tel No . . . .

Email . . . .

Valid to 31/12/05

Would you like to find out more about Francis Frith?

We have recently recruited some entertaining speakers who are happy to visit local groups, clubs and societies to give an illustrated talk documenting Frith's travels and photographs. If you are a member of such a group and are interested in hosting a presentation, we would love to hear from you.

Our speakers bring with them a small selection of our local town and county books, together with sample prints. They are happy to take orders. A small proportion of the order value is donated to the group who have hosted the presentation. The talks are therefore an excellent way of fundraising for small groups and societies.

Can you help us with information about any of the Frith photographs in this book?

We are gradually compiling an historical record for each of the photographs in the Frith archive. It is always fascinating to find out the names of the people shown in the pictures, as well as insights into the shops, buildings and other features depicted.

If you recognize anyone in the photographs in this book, or if you have information not already included in the author's caption, do let us know. We would love to hear from you, and will try to publish it in future books or articles.

Our production team

Frith books are produced by a small dedicated team at offices in the converted Grade II listed 18th-century barn at Teffont near Salisbury, illustrated above. Most have worked with the Frith Collection for many years. All have in common one quality: they have a passion for the Frith Collection. The team is constantly expanding, but currently includes:

Jason Buck, John Buck, Ruth Butler, Heather Crisp, Isobel Hall, Julian Hight, Peter Horne, James Kinnear, Karen Kinnear, Tina Leary, David Marsh, Sue Molloy, Kate Rotondetto, Dean Scource, Eliza Sackett, Terence Sackett, Sandra Sampson, Adrian Sanders, Sandra Sanger, Julia Skinner, Lewis Taylor, Shelley Tolcher and Lorraine Tuck.